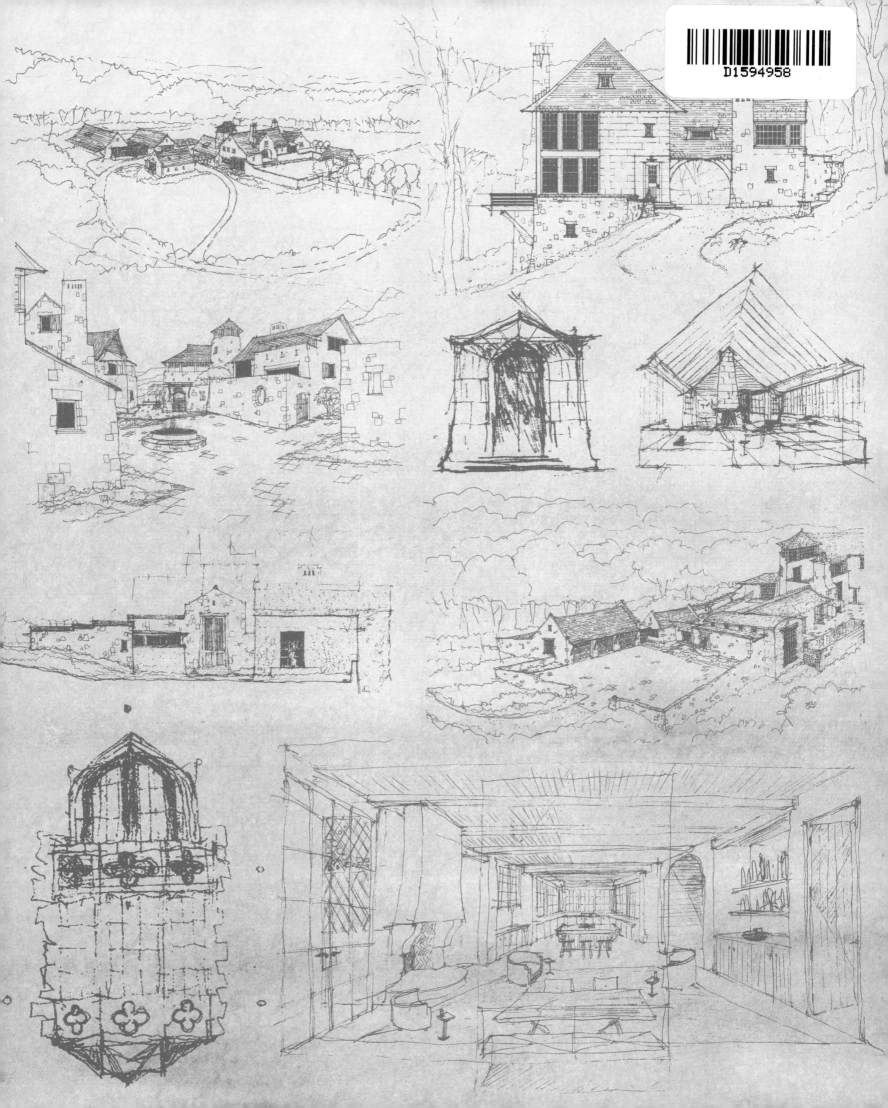

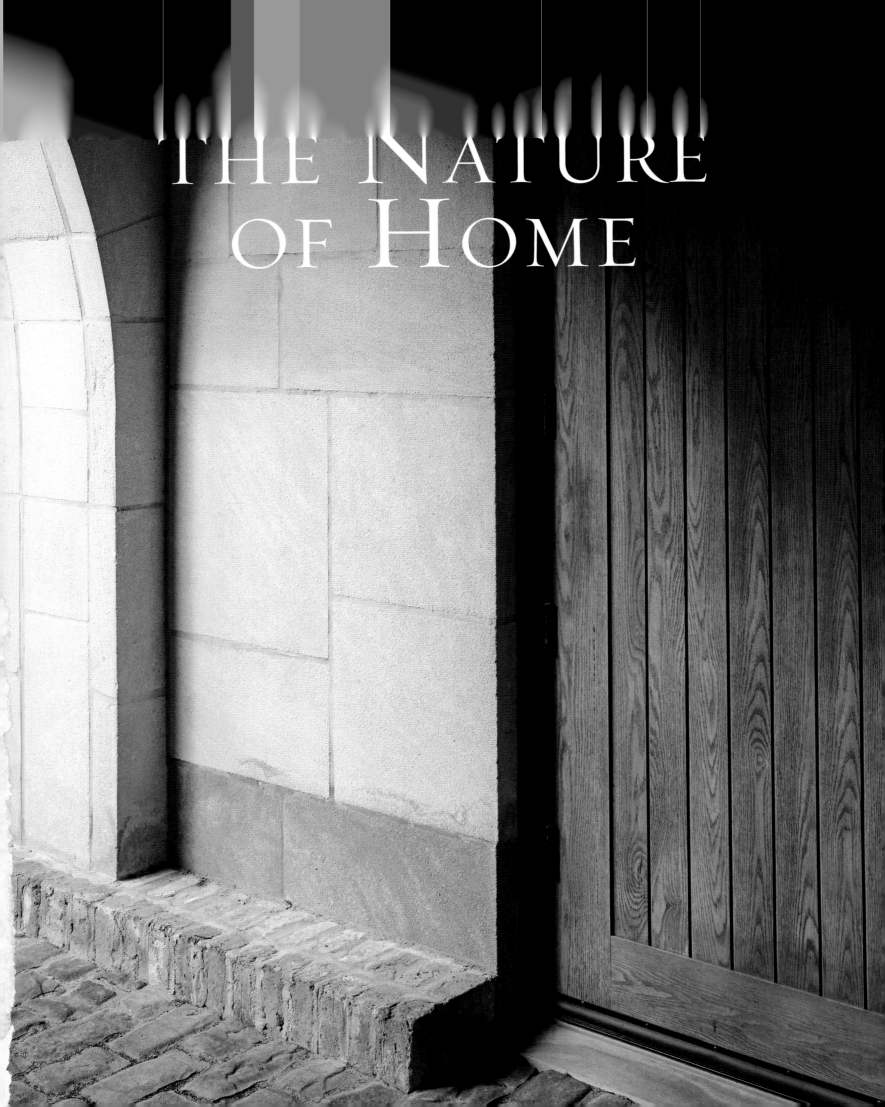

THE NATURE OF HOME

THE NATURE OF HOME

CREATING TIMELESS HOUSES

JEFFREY DUNGAN

PHOTOGRAPHY BY WILLIAM ABRANOWICZ

RIZZOLI
NEW YORK

New York Paris London Milan

To my beautiful daughters,
Hannah, Emma Grace, and Tate

CONTENTS

INTRODUCTION

John Muir's belief that "the clearest way into the Universe is through a forest wilderness" has always struck a deep chord within me. I, too, feel the momentum of the Earth and its power to bring us to the light of the divine. Perhaps this is because I grew up on a family farm surrounded by the rolling fields of St. Clair County, Alabama, with the woods close by. In the days before my responsibilities on the farm were more pressing, I would wake up early and venture out with my dog into the mysterious landscape beyond our threshold. Out there I was alone, yet not lonely, surrounded by the quiet majesty and vast power of nature. In the flat hollows of the deep woods, the oaks stood before me like giant columns. Sunlight barely filtered through the layers of the boughs, so not much undergrowth could develop—just moss, leaves, and the shifting, dappled patterns over old logging pathways.

I became steeped in the spaces I explored, and educated by them, too. The wisdom of the trees seemed to get inside of me. Years later, I realized that I was drawing inspiration from their memory. Those oaks—huge, with glorious arms outstretched to the sky—taught me about elegance and verticality. The sweep of their trunks—broad at the base, tapering gradually upward into the higher reaches—has influenced much of my design thinking. They became the basis of some of my forms, the chimneys, exterior walls, and roofs with profiles and textures that appear closer to nature than to anything made by man. They are the inspiration for the soulful, artful, earthy homes and interiors that we try to create, places imbued with spirit and emotions emanating from deep within, from memories of my first love and mentor, the agrarian, bucolic landscape of my youth.

I was also influenced by many people, in particular my grandfather, born in 1899, who was old-school to say the least. He taught me how to do work—real work. A bit stoic, he didn't allow much talking while he instructed me in the ways of handling animals and sling blades. When he did speak, he passed along deep truths that became part of the very fiber of my being, truths that seem beyond the beginnings of my memory. My dad, among many things, taught me to get along with everyone, having never met a stranger himself. My mom taught me that education was each person's first job. She also encouraged me in painting and the arts. Without her urging, in no way would I have become an architect.

The beauty of mystery calls in the misty morning at the edge of pinewoods
and fields of a farm property we designed in the deep South.

As a youngster, I was fascinated with drawing and sketching, which led to painting in watercolor and oil, plus a love of art that abides to this day. It was in many ways a natural progression for me to become interested in architecture. Years later, after graduating from Auburn University's renowned architecture program, I took my first steps into the profession at a small residential firm that allowed me a wide variety of unique design opportunities and challenges. Intensely interested in the art of creation and the act of construction, I gained valuable experiences working with people and learning how the industry functioned over the next decade. On February 14, 1999, I decided to strike out on my own with my great friend, the talented architect Louis Nequette. We worked out of a small sunroom-cum-studio in Louis's classic, 1920s-era apartment, with no comprehension of what we had embarked upon. We had a handful of projects and a burning desire to pursue the architect's craft of realizing beauty with thoughtfulness, care, and passion. While Louis and I decided to take different trajectories years ago, we remain to this day great friends and brothers in the fight against ugliness in the world.

We started out with a feeling of kinship with the Arts and Crafts period, celebrating creativity as a way of life rather than a style. I have always hoped, like the heroes of that movement, to enrich people's day-to-day existence by making truly inspired places for them to live. No matter where you are in the world, you spend most of your time in environments designed by another human being. What drives me is a desire for people to know that the person who created these places cared deeply about the way they experience them. I want the spaces I design to create an emotional response, to spark thought, to encourage relaxation, and, above all, to endure in a timeless way.

In order to stir people, architecture must have rhythm and harmony akin to music. It should have the passion of an aria and the power of beauty. The tools we wield to deliver this kind of emotional impact are light, proportion, materials, structure, opacity, and transparency, to name a few. These are some of the elements in design, which we use to create the desired emotional effect. Such expressive environments are not easily made, nor are they the work of just one person. Each takes the efforts of many dedicated, talented people. At the beginning, there is only the purity of the idea, nascent in the mind. Then that becomes a dream, which begins to create a vision. The magical moment is when the end of a pencil conveys that vision onto a napkin, an envelope, or paper plate. It emerges out of the ether and into the world. A house is *born* in a way, and to witness that occurrence is creative bliss.

The design of every house is a journey for the imagination, so with each I try to do one thing that I have never done before. I enjoy drawing a house as *it wants to be*, knitting the site and its owner into a setting in which they can both live happily. My bent towards remaining curious and innovative—and the differing personas of each client and site—combine to make each project its own totally unique adventure. In many ways, designing a house is really just an excuse for a relationship. And like a relationship, the design for a house always evolves.

Some things, however, stay the same. There are many things in life we want our houses to insulate us from, like the cold north winds of winter, the hot Southern sun, or the natural violence of thunderstorms. More than this, we hope for a home to be a citadel to protect us from life's pressures, a bulwark and a comfort against the tests of time and the stresses of life. In a place that feels permanent, that bears an air of lasting beauty, lies what we mean by the term *timeless*.

John Ruskin said, "When we build, let us think that we build forever." A timeless house speaks of authenticity, character, and lived history that reveals itself through the natural patinas that come with age. Authenticity is important, because it seems in such short supply in our fast-paced world. It's there in buildings that have lasted because they were well-constructed, that have endured also because their owners treasured them and preserved them as heirlooms for their family and generations to come. Timelessness may be a quality difficult to define, but we know it when we see it. It has to do with honesty and integrity it is immune to the changes and evolutions of fashion and trends—it's classic.

When I graduated from college, I was fully prepared to "scare the world with a new architecture." After I finished a few houses, the only person I had scared was myself. I went back to the drawing board. During that time, I became twice the student of history that I had been. In history, I found mentors who continue to influence and inspire me, among them Charles Voysey, Sir Edwin Lutyens, and Carlo Scarpa. My favorite was and remains the ascetic Voysey, whose advice to "look at no ugly thing twice" I still try to heed.

The more I learn from architecture's past, the more I want to design places that simultaneously stretch through time backward and forward, that give a nod to history and yet have a foot firmly in the modern day. In our office, we try to take the best of what we glean from historical references and make homes that are livable for our times. We envision these as being heirloom houses—clean-lined and simple, made of materials that revel in their age—being handed down to future generations. We focus on how our clients want to live, and make design decisions based on their dreams. In thinking differently and taking a longer view, we inevitably end up with a uniquely personal answer and an environment that is transformative for those who live in it.

Most days, I pinch myself that I live the life I do. Our projects take me across the country and to other countries and continents. I am thrilled by collaborations with talented interior designers of vision and impeccable taste. I am amazed watching the capable hands of artisans, carpenters who sew beams together like thread, blacksmiths bending hot metal, masons chipping away at stone—the list goes on. I'm inspired and humbled by the creative people in our studio—many of whom have been toiling away with me for more than a decade or two—and the passionate banter we have, sharing ideas and arguing about the best way to make these ideas real. Over hundreds of projects, we have developed our own shorthand language. What we create together is magical and fulfilling to me, because it is better than what any one of us could achieve on our own.

While we evolve, we still hold fast to certain eternal truths like simplicity, elegance, and comfort. What has not changed since we opened our studio almost twenty years ago is a love of simplicity, or at least the *idea* of simplicity—yet simple carries with it its own complexity. I also love elegance, and while I know that simple is elegant, it *is* the elegant that makes us feel elevated just by being in its presence. As a designer, I know how rare a feat simplicity is to achieve—but it is always a feat worth attempting. For the record, though, my personal style is always about comfort. Only when we are comfortable in the spaces we inhabit can we become our best selves.

What I hope most is for the houses we design to affect people in an inspiring way and to help them live a life beyond their dreams. That's an ambitious and audacious goal, but I know that design has that kind of power. A house says things about us whether we like it or not. I want the houses we design to say the right things about the people who live in them. I try intuitively to understand our clients, to comprehend the deeper meaning in what they say and what is unspoken. What is the essence of these people? What are their values? I listen to their desires for the home. I begin to envision a trajectory for the design that would render shape and form to best express them as they truly are. If I understand them from the beginning, the design happens in an almost effortless way. In the end, there will be something standing that could cast a shadow for centuries, telling their story.

Simplicity and comfort in the stone base and wooden
siding of a lake house guestroom wing.

THE LAND

I have had a lifelong love affair with the land. It isn't something you learn from books. As far as I can tell, the feeling is steeped into me from my experiences of youth on a farm. For me, the land has a powerful momentum. It creates drama with its views. It rolls. It rises. It falls. In life, I cannot ignore it. In architecture, I must honor it.

Practically from the dawn of time, our history and mythology have emphasized our deep connection with the land. In the biblical Genesis story, the first man was called Adam. The corresponding word for earth in Hebrew is *Adamah*. The close linguistic relationship emphasizes the inextricable link between humankind and the ground that sustains us. Our ties to the earth seem to have frayed as we have moved from an agrarian culture to a progressively more urban, industrial, and technological one. But the cord is long and soulful, and we can never cut it completely. It's there, in the awe we feel at the power of the Grand Canyon, the beauty of a fairway at Augusta, the majesty of the Blue Ridge Mountains, or the simple elegance of the ocean's long horizon.

The first goal of my creative process is always to understand what the land is doing at the particular spot we call the site. Be it steep or flat, heavily forested or wide open, the site has undulations, a trajectory of the

There's inspiration in the form of thousands of acres of rolling hills. On this horse farm outside Montgomery, Alabama, the rail fence inspired the railing we used on the house.

15

The movement of this site—the rise and fall of its lakeside terrain—provided cues for rooflines that gently step down to the water's edge.

sun, and other inherent features that are like reading tea leaves to determine how best to fit the structure into the perfect location. Always, my desire is for the house to merge with the earth to form a new expression, one where both the man-made and God-made become one.

On any site, I am always interested in what we can celebrate in the views it affords us. There are views we want to capture as well as those we want to avoid. I am continually searching for a sweet spot where the views are best and the topography is amenable, even welcoming, to a structure. Walking around the site, the discovery of its sweet spot is immediate and profound. This is a magical kind of experience. Upon further investigation, it begins to become more clear how the house would lay itself out: the approach, the point of arrival, and where the major rooms would want to be to take the best advantage of the views. In my mind, the house just lays itself out on the site like a cloth draped across the earth.

The architecture should in some way relate to the colors and textures of the landscape in its materials, details, and overall attitude—by which I mean the variety of experiences that comes with different contexts. A flat, sandy site with palmettos and live oaks facing the ocean's horizon line obviously looks and feels very different than a hillside site at the edge of a sheer stone cliff with mountain views that take in rocky terrain all around. I take cues from the immediate surroundings, but I absorb the overall vibe of the scene too, attempting to make an acceptable and appropriate response to the terrain.

They say you only get one chance at a first impression. The same goes for anything we design and build, especially something as epic and enduring as a house. It is critical that the architecture is deserving of its environment. A home at peace with its surroundings will always be superior to one that is not. The best compliment I can ever receive is that a house we designed looked as if it had grown out of the site or had always been there.

Nature's serenity provides its own healing reward, as in the sweeping view from
this project at Lake Martin, Alabama, punctuated by islands covered in cedar trees.
To harmonize with the site, we used cedar for the dock as well as the house.

PREVIOUS PAGES: Working in
many locations around the
country allows for designs
influenced by unique
ecosystems. We often borrow
from the indigenous terroir and
its feeling, or we contrast it
intentionally to form a thoughtful
composition. RIGHT: We
designed this house in a piano
noble fashion to make the most
of spectacular views of the
ocean, rendering the upper
level in a range of colors similar
to the pines resting on
a plinth of contrasting stucco.

PREVIOUS PAGES: Against the long horizon line of the Gulf of Mexico, a sweeping view of dunes and clumps of palmettos creates a visually placid environment. For the house on this site, we designed an architecture that responds to the landscape of the shore with simple forms and white stucco walls to protect from the summer sun. RIGHT: Nothing says the South quite as much as moss-covered oak trees dotted along a rolling countryside. The shuttered porch overlooks a grouping of chairs turned toward the sunset.

LA PETITE MAISON

Design is really a search for limits. Sometimes, counterintuitively perhaps, the limitations actually come in handy. They certainly did in the case of this one-story, two-bedroom, European-inspired cottage in Mountain Brook, Alabama, for clients who were ready to downsize.

Years ago, we had worked with this couple on extensive renovations and additions to a historic English Tudor home. After many happy years there, having bought a tiny piece of property in a wonderful nearby neighborhood, they planned to give the big house to their son and his growing family. Their new lot's diminutive dimensions made any number of design decisions much more straightforward, because instead of accommodating three good ways to lay out the house properly, there was room for just one.

These clients have always appreciated well-made, simple design and all things of character and patina, especially those that have stood the test of time in an elegant way. He worked in an architecture firm as a college student and had become fascinated by construction means and methods. A fine-art lover and very good abstract painter herself, she had a vision also for her interiors. These two were not the whatever-the-architect-says types. They had strong opinions, and they had ideas. As I listened to their comments and opinions, I worked hard to keep the design understated and create a house that looked like it had been there for decades.

One stroke of divine design fortune had to do with the roof. I wanted it to look like it didn't care what anyone thought about it, to be something unique that made a statement all by itself, so the predictable roof materials would not do. Searching for something different, we found a clay-tile roof from an old Spanish convent. When we got the samples, it was instantly a done deal. We had the roof tiles shipped over in a container, hoping it would make it through customs in time to fit into the construction schedule.

We wanted something special for the roof of this house. We knew these antique terra-cotta tiles salvaged from a Spanish convent were perfect the instant we saw the samples. My favorites are the curved, "bonnet"-shaped pieces, which form the corners of the hipped roof.

I have found that a simple palette of materials makes for the best compositions. Details add another layer. To create rhythm and definition on the facade, we used limestone surrounds at the windows and corbeled the stone out like a shelf to support the copper ogee-shaped gutters.

To comply with the husband's bent toward bulletproof construction, we made the exterior walls thick. Then we made them even thicker and structured them out of concrete. Their massiveness (more than twenty inches deep) allowed us to play with scooping out the interior walls to create windows reminiscent of medieval castles.

The floor plan was the picture of simplicity. With only five rooms on the entry level, each had its own story and vibe. The living room, for example, was based on the idea of a French salon, traditionally a space for greeting guests before they came into the rest of a much larger, grander house; it has a curved ceiling to provide a welcoming embrace. The den was really a retreat, so we gave it very cozy timbers and created a loft to make a little bookish getaway. My personal favorite was the glassed-in conservatory, which in such a petite house doubled as the boot room and everyday entry as well as a flower-arranging and catchall space.

I limited the interior materials to three: plaster, wood, and stone. Stone on the inside was important in order to have continuity with the exterior, like houses from the past. To complete this thought, we created the conservatory space that plays with the memory of older houses that evolved over time, those where a terrace, a porch, or a storage space had been "taken in" to create another room. Good design has always been about illusion.

And details matter. The hallway has vaulted and curved ceilings, groin vaults soaring overhead. We brought in timber framers from Maine to create the den's heavy, exposed woodwork and a blacksmith to forge the metal handrails. Like a bar in a classic French bistro (think Balthazar in Manhattan), the kitchen countertops here are of sturdy, old-school pewter with a thick, easy-to-cozy-up-to edge and a rich, dull sheen. One of my favorite aspects of being involved in the construction process is the edits and changes we make on the fly. Much of the final detailing here was done in situ, drawing on walls and timbers directly with carpenter pencils, collaborating over the nuances with the artisans as they practiced their crafts.

Sometimes great things come in small packages. I always encourage my clients not to make houses larger than they need to be, so that we can make the quality as high as possible. Like an espresso instead of a coffee, this little house is the perfect example of the power of that idea.

Patina is important in creating a house with an enduring appearance.
Here, we used antiqued limestone steps and quoins to further the feeling
of age for a home that looks like it has been there for decades.

ABOVE: Anchoring the sunken garden, we made a fountain from an old millstone and a limestone urn. OPPOSITE: The conservatory's steel windows enclose stone walls, suggesting an older outdoor space that's been enclosed to create another room.
Paige Sumblin Schnell, the interior designer on this project, hung an eighteenth-century Piedmontese luster lantern in the hall.

PREVIOUS PAGES: The living room's bronze-and-glass railing allows a greater view outside and invites further exploring downstairs. OPPOSITE: Created in situ, this hammered-iron stair railing is saddle-mounted to oak stringers. ABOVE: Antique oak beams were hewn to fit the loft's roofline. FOLLOWING PAGES: Pewter countertops and French limestone floors introduce a sense of age to the kitchen.

PAGE 42: A small space like this breakfast nook feels great alone and fun with friends. PAGE 43: The conservatory makes a cozy, everyday entry. PREVIOUS PAGES: Details—limestone portals, stone corbeled eaves, herringbone patterns—give the eye places to go. ABOVE: An antique wood frieze is a beautiful contrast to the sleek marble bathroom. OPPOSITE: A bed nook in the master bedroom balances the vaulted ceiling.

LIGHT

In thinking about light—that magical material that renders us the world—my mind goes deep into the essence of things. Light gives us shadows and highlights. It reveals shape and form. Without it there would be no life, for almost nothing in nature grows in its absence.

Through the ages poets, philosophers, scientists, and artists have all espoused light's inspirational, ethereal, and transformational qualities. Their writings on the topic bring its meaning powerfully home to me. Two are especially close to my heart, as they illuminate the truth about the fundamental importance of light to architecture. The first—"Live in rooms filled with light"—hails from Aulus Cornelius Celsus, a Roman encyclopedist from the first century A.D. whose one surviving work, *De Medicina*, offers practical advice on leading a healthy lifestyle. The second—"I sense Light as the giver of all presences, and material as spent Light. What is made by Light casts a shadow, and the shadow belongs to Light"—is from one of our greatest poet-architects, Louis Kahn.

When we begin our design work and first visit the site, I start to consider straightaway how the house can best fit into that unique environment.

Light and shadow in a stairwell of wooden planks. Window panes are projected onto the wall boards forming new patterns.

Understanding the arc of the sun's path across what we will build is critical to the process of determining how best to place and lay out the architecture. That same knowledge affects the organization of the interiors in a pivotal way, for it will define everything from how gently the homeowners will wake up in the morning to whether or not their rooms will still be enjoyable when they have the heat of western or southern exposures. By contrast, northern light is wonderful because it carries no heat, being reflected rather than direct light. Southern light is powerful, yet more easily controllable (by careful design of eaves or overhangs) than eastern or western light.

Porches and pergolas that screen the sun are favorite devices with southern exposures, especially when they have overhanging eaves deep enough to allow low-trajectory winter sun to flood the space while keeping the higher-angled summer sun at bay. This is not some new idea, but a strategy gleaned from the history of design in eras before we became so dependent on the luxury of mechanical systems to make our homes comfortable. It remains good practice to abide by such principles. And I believe it makes the interiors more usable and their light more enjoyable.

Perhaps some things are fascinating only to architects, but light is meaningful and powerful and worth the thoughtful effort to capture and employ in our homes. Its effect on our lives and influence on our moods is incalculable. For along with all its other properties, light imbues us with joy.

When an architect arranges a house thoughtfully in nature, the result is rooms bathed in natural, life-enhancing light over the course of each day and through the seasons. As I sit at my desk writing these words, the morning's sunbeams are flowing in onto the paper through the windowpanes, casting a grid of slender shadows from the muntins. As I move my pencil over the paper, I am part of an illuminated rhythm of white, then charcoal gray, then light again—almost musical, sublime, magical, and ethereal.

OPPOSITE: Sleeping on a lakeside screened porch is almost like camping out. Early morning sunbeams streaming onto its bluestone pavers bring the space alive.
FOLLOWING PAGES: Light is architecture's perfect partner and muse. We celebrate it in a stairwell, frame it with arches, or playfully tease it with tiny peek holes.

Light plays. It's important to change colors, materials, and finishes from sheer to matte to shiny in order to appreciate light's varying personas.

Light streaming in from above is powerful. In spaces that allow for openings on high, like this one we made for my friend, designer Richard Tubb, it makes for a wonderful ambience.

Nowhere is the daylight brighter and more pervasive than in Florida, where the shadows are just as poignant and ever changing as the sand on the beaches. The limestone-and-cypress balcony of a house in Alys Beach is a canvas reflecting the sky's infinite moods.

THE BEACH HOUSE

The beach is a special place that holds memories of summer joys, where the endless horizon of ocean reminds us of the eternal. Ironically, it's as physically toxic a construction environment as exists anywhere—a combination of beauty for everyone else and beast for the builder and architect. Even so, creating a house at the beach is a chance to design an escape. For what is the beach if not that?

One day, some old friends called to discuss their dreams of building a house at the beach in Florida. We had done a house together twenty years earlier and I had a satellite office at the beach, so they asked me to guide them to the right property. There was a piece of property at Alys Beach that I had long admired; it looked out over a gorgeous public green where outdoor weddings are held and possessed amazing views of the Gulf of Mexico just beyond the dunes. A diminutive size of forty feet by forty feet, the lot was also quite a challenge. The clients said all they wanted were three bedrooms, a pool, a two-car garage, and a few other outdoor spaces—plus, I assumed, a kitchen. The garage alone took up one-third of the site. So I said, "No problem."

If necessity is the mother of invention, this house was going to be something more like a magic trick of the vertical kind. The obvious place to begin was with the basics of program and site. I quickly saw the design would involve a lot of weaving areas together in a much tighter way than normal. So

OPPOSITE: The beautiful seaside village of Alys Beach, Florida, makes the perfect setting for a Moorish-inspired jewel box of high, white stucco walls and black-framed windows.
FOLLOWING PAGES: The exterior stair cantilevers off the third story (pictured on page 77). Using plaster and wood, I wanted to create an interior stair with a similar feeling.

OPPOSITE: The curved profile of a service stair inside the Arc de Triomphe in Paris inspired this railing. ABOVE LEFT: Antique oak beams from old cotton gins meet the Venetian plaster on the underside of the cantilevered stair. ABOVE RIGHT: A fan of Spanish architecture thanks to multiple trips to Barcelona, I see the Moorish influences in these harlequin-patterned windowpanes.

tight, in fact, that counterintuitive thoughts—like hanging the stairs to a rooftop aerie off the side of the house, for instance—started to actually make sense.

To create privacy in such a tight-knit place was very important. Since the floor plan would be so snug, I made a point of having one bedroom on each floor, which solved the privacy issue in some ways. This also left a fourth floor to provide the catbird-seat view out over the beach. The interior stairs and an elevator became focal points in such a vertical arrangement.

What became enthralling to me was how to articulate the verticality in an elegant way. I was long ago inspired by the idea of a "strong tower" and heavily influenced by those the Irish built for avoiding marauding invaders. The baroque architecture of Barcelona, with its Moorish and Gothic notes, was also lurking in my subconscious. Combining these heavy masonries in some beachy way held a mystery that was intoxicating for me. Our thickened concrete walls became a kind of veil, creating a buffer from the sun and giving privacy to the interior spaces. The unique entry is a zaguan: an elaborate, unconditioned barrel-vaulted passage into the interior courtyard and pool from grand old colonial homes in Spain.

On the inside, we kept the white-stucco language of the exterior by using Venetian plaster. White and black together have always been powerful, so we painted the windows black and the railings as well, to provide contrast.

Some houses seem to have an idea of what they want to be all by themselves. In the end, this house was one of those combinations of necessity and imagination, of logic and fantasy. Never before had a house said to me, "Look, just put the stairs outside and hang them off the wall. We don't have any more room inside here." I listened. And the act of climbing the almost one hundred exterior steps, supported by curving, swirling concrete, is a transformative experience, one that brings you up and out into the salty air to a view of that eternal line of ocean, a reminder of why the beach always beckons.

At the ceiling of the master bedroom, the harlequin pattern used for the windows of the master bath repeats in Venetian plaster. Interior designer Ashley Garrison chose furnishings and fabrics in keeping with the architectural theme of white materials and clean lines.

OPPOSITE: For me, the beach means softness—water, breezes, sand—and sea-kissed materials like driftwood. Wanting that feeling in the kitchen, the builder and I collaborated to create slightly cerused oak panels for the cabinetry. ABOVE: We designed an adjacent dining booth and console in creamy white leather with Grant Trick, my main man and design muse for all things fabric or upholstered.

ABOVE: Alone at the very top, the master suite enjoys some of the best views of the beaches and dunes of the Gulf of Mexico. OPPOSITE: We liked the cerused treatment of the kitchen cabinetry so much, we used it in other places, like baths and doors, to keep the detailing in the house consistent and simple.

This is the view down from the second-floor guest bedroom into what I call the grotto. The calming sound of water echoes in other spaces throughout the house and reverberates outward to the entry. The ground-floor bedroom opens directly onto this pool for private late-night dips.

ABOVE: A Moorish-inspired arch and open-air gate lead into a zaguan entry that frames the view terminating at the pool and offers an invitation to relax. OPPOSITE: One of my favorite details of this house is the cantilevered concrete stair to the rooftop terrace.

The climb's reward is a view of
the public green and beach entry
unlike any other in Alys Beach.

ELLIOTT ERWITT PERSONAL BEST

MATERIALS

A friend told me years ago that "authenticity is the new luxury." I don't think it's any less true today. I have found that the fewer materials shaping a room, the more quiet a room becomes. I'm drawn to materials that are honest and help us feel grounded. Stone, wood, plaster, and copper—the substances I love to build with—are the architectural soul mates of light. What I desire is to find and celebrate what is real, true, and honest.

I love natural materials that are articulated in an unadorned way and displayed in the light. Materials give us texture, color, and depth. They can be slick, sleek, and sophisticated or deep, rich, and luxurious. They can be heavy and ancient or light and airy, but just as powerful. Our material choices convey so much about what we want to say in a home or a room. Simple places should have a simple palette of materials. If we want to be refined and elegant, we may head toward marble, Venetian plaster, or glass. When our desire is for a more rustic character, sawn wood, fieldstone, and patinated copper top our list. Entire styles of architecture revolve around certain materials. Imagine a Gothic building without stone or a Tudor house sans brick and half-timbers. Spanish and Italian architecture are wrapped in stucco. Carpenter Gothic is rendered in wood by definition.

When considering selections for interiors, the conversation becomes deeper, more intimate, and more emotional. Interiors are where we live, and we are in more personal contact with the physicality of the surroundings. I

OPPOSITE: Contrasting textures—here, Tennessee fieldstone, smooth limestone, and planked southern pine—make the perfect backdrop for softer things like linen and suede. FOLLOWING PAGES, LEFT: From the front door to the interior, materials establish the mood. FOLLOWING PAGES, RIGHT: I love how the dark pockets in the wood harmonize with the blackness of hammered-iron stair railings.

think because of this, and because the interiors are protected from the whims of the weather, our palette of materials seems to increase exponentially.

To create the right mood or feeling, we have to make the right choices and thoughtful selections. It's not easy. In our work, we get to design both interiors and exteriors. It has been and continues to be a fascination of mine to see the use of materials at both extremes. The same west-facing exterior wall (think harsh summer sun), for example, could on its interior face be the headboard wall in a master bedroom. There couldn't be two more different surfaces, and yet it is the materiality of each that defines their function and ultimate success. Stone or masonry would be a good exterior choice to protect the inside from heat transfer; on the interior, I would use a fabric on the walls to soften the room and give it a more comfortable, relaxed texture.

In general, the exterior materials are the heavy lifters. As such, they need to be robust and protective to stand up to nature's abuse and the test of time. Inside, where more delicate materials often prevail, we select finishes for which we search the world over. Marble, for example, is quarried from deep in the earth then shipped across oceans. It comes in all kinds of colors as well as the patterning we call "movement" from natural veining and texture. Then there is the finish, from polished to honed or leathered. Floors of hardwood introduce all kinds of earthy colors and textures also, depending on whether they are smooth or circle-sawn or even hand-scraped with an ancient tool called an adze. And oh, the rich history of reclaimed materials and the stories they tell. Like pecky cypress: dredged up from the bottom of rivers and swamps, not having seen the light of day for perhaps a century or two, it captivates us with its indentations, apertures, and stippled grain.

In the hands of thoughtful artisans, materials—Louis Kahn's "spent light"— inspire us, move us, and enrich our lives.

OPPOSITE: Many things define an interior, but none are more all-encompassing than flooring. In some houses, especially where weekend and vacation use are the mainstay, it is wonderful to go with a less fussy feel, like these circle-sawn planks of old pine, which are almost as indestructible as they are beautiful. FOLLOWING PAGES: Each material evokes a certain feeling; the smooth plaster stairs create a sophisticated air, while natural stone and oak beams elicit a more earthy and rustic mood.

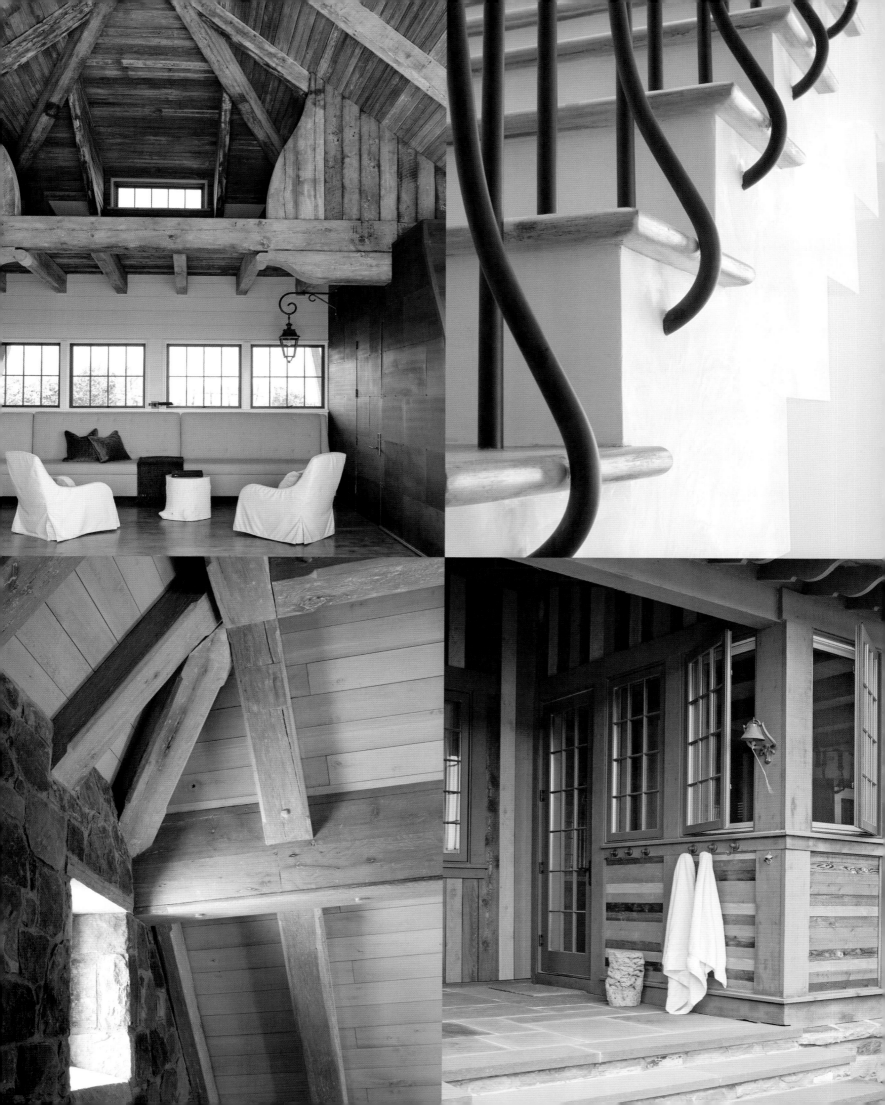

THE FARMHOUSE

I grew up on a farm. And of course, now I miss it. So when an opportunity came along to work on a project involving a large farm—a 3,000-acre weekend retreat in Lowndesboro, Alabama—I had more than a passing interest. The client's family and extended family loved to enjoy its wide-open spaces, riding horses, hunting (their bird dogs always in tow), fishing, tending a large garden, and cooking. When we began, all that stood on the property was a horse barn and a small cabin they had drafted themselves and built with the help of their farmhands. They had large dreams, though, wanting to make the property into an heirloom for their sons and their extended families.

I wanted to honor the little cabin. Still, I knew it had to be transformed. I soon realized that instead of editing what was there (a strategy that wasn't working), it made more sense to engulf it within the additional spaces they had asked for, creating a new architecture of porches, kitchen, and bedrooms. This scheme formed a double *L* shape that created an indoor/outdoor lifestyle of porches and courtyards defined by the house and landscaping.

OPPOSITE: The "bunkhouse," a large entertaining space with two bedrooms, is attached to the main house with long, wide porches. Patty, the owners' bird dog, always welcomes guests and hunters back to the house. FOLLOWING PAGES: I have a deep appreciation for old farms and how they have been added to over time; we wanted to create a compound of buildings to mimic that same sense of history.

One of the most interesting things about farmhouses is how they grow over time. They grow in porches, dogtrots, and shed roofs. They grow because the family grows. Growth is the whole reason farms exist. To celebrate that idea, we designed the house with a series of interwoven rooflines accentuated by cedar shakes, the perfect salt-and-pepper textured beard. This intentionally wonky sculpture of roofs gave the place an informal air and a camp-like feel.

It made sense to use rugged, rustic materials that were bulletproof, dog-proof, kid-proof, and party-proof. The lady of the house initially felt stone was too heavy, and maybe too serious, for a farmhouse. She ultimately agreed to use stone for a column or two and as a base below the porch floorboards. However, once she saw the stonework, as adamant as she had been against the stone before, she became just as passionate to have more of it—which was my wish as well.

We felt free to let the rusticity of the materials flow into the interiors. The exterior stone entered the rooms through the five fireplaces. We brought in weathered beams, repurposed from old Southern cotton gins, that made great trusses and railings. Circle-sawn floorboards that no dog could destroy were perfect for the desired texture and appropriate for the necessary resiliency of such a place.

Probably my favorite room was the new kitchen, added to the rear of the house. After a long struggle to unify the existing and new rooflines, it became clear that the best answer was to separate them altogether. The result of this decision created a kitchen with a fourteen-foot-high ceiling. Taking the contrast between new and old a step further, we enclosed the kitchen with windows from countertop to ceiling, creating a space we could not have anticipated, much like the new house itself. The outcome in the end was happy and serendipitous, a family farm appearing to have grown just where it was planted.

OPPOSITE: Stone porch columns and brooding, protective eaves with decorative rafter tails and pine decking are architecture at its most basic. FOLLOWING PAGES, LEFT: The porches weave the compound together; they also make great entertaining spaces. FOLLOWING PAGES, RIGHT: Antique collected pieces sit quietly waiting for the next gathering of hunters.

ABOVE: Timber ceiling joists meet stone at the fireplace edge. OPPOSITE: Low ceilings make for a cozy, intimate conversation area by the fireplace; vaulted ceilings with dormers create a neighboring space for large groups. FOLLOWING PAGES: A shuttered porch off the master bedroom is a great spot for an afternoon nap.

ABOVE: The horse-fence motif inspired this handrail of reclaimed oak.
OPPOSITE: We made this high-ceilinged kitchen with windows on three
sides for our hunter-gatherer-type clients who love the outdoors.

I think that rooms should elicit emotional and visceral responses from us. More than anything else, it is a feeling we are designing.

Antique timbers frame the fireplace in the master bedroom.

ABOVE: In this detail of the fireplace mantel, you can see a play of textures in wood and stone. OPPOSITE: One of the main entries into the house, this screened porch expands into the original living room, forming a merging of inside and outside. FOLLOWING PAGES: Nature's influence and pull is inescapable: pine thickets and fields make for cypress tables, trusses, and high ceilings.

STONE

Rocks and their formations speak to the beginning, to the ancient and the prehistoric, to what it really means to endure, and in some ways to the eternal. In so doing they evoke respect, for compared to the human life span, they enjoy a quasi-immortality. The still-standing ruins of previous civilizations suggest, at least intuitively, that any structure we build of stone might have a chance to stand for another millennium or more—a consolation of sorts for time's relentlessness and our own mortality.

Over the years, I have studied and collected all kinds of rocks and minerals, geodes and semiprecious quartzes, everything from sulfur to pumice to pyrite. Even today, stones of all kinds sit on my desk, simply because they make me happy. Many of my clients feel the same way. As one of them once said during a presentation, "You had me at stone."

What draws us to fieldstone, marble, limestone, and their igneous and volcanic cousins may be the same quality that appeals to us in those people who appear unfazed and carry on even as age exacts its toll on their visage. We value rugged authenticity in a face. When we see a weathered stone facade, we feel its security, its power to shield us from the vagaries of the climate and the uncertainty of the outside world.

OPPOSITE: Soft light spreads from the window across a wall of ashlar-cut stone onto limestone pavers; in the foreground is a limestone fireplace surround. FOLLOWING PAGES: The texture of stone can be quite varied to reflect its intended use: sanded smooth for surfaces touched often and rougher and more natural for others less close at hand.

There are so many kinds of stone, as many as there are faces. In pattern, hue, and texture, geology has produced a countless number of options. Sandstone typically has a wonderfully stippled texture. It comes in colors like khaki, ocher, subtle pink, and even peach. Limestone tends to range in palette from grays into the nutty browns, which can vary further when cut, shaped, and finished. Fieldstone renders itself at home almost anywhere because it is offers a quintessentially local, indigenous facade that instantly looks at home in its surroundings. Moss rock from streams or rivers and ancient coral rock formed in the ocean introduce a sense of color and context, blending almost perfectly with their waterside environment.

Then there is the fabrication and finishing—the cutting, patterning, piecing, polishing. From the integrity of piled-up stones and boulders to the finely dressed regimentation of ashlar masonry to the finesse of perfectly polished slabs, the options are endless. Randomly sized rectangles of the ashlar pattern are a personal favorite because they have a studied nonchalance and impress without appearing to try too hard or be too formal. More informal still is river rock, rounded and organic. Dressier by nature is coursed limestone, particularly in a brick pattern. And there are variations on every single one of those themes. Add in the permutations of mortar, which possesses its own spectrum of color, texture, and composition. Then factor in the narrowness or width of the interstices it fills and the way it is squished, brushed, or tooled into those spaces. A dizzying, sometimes intimidating infinity of design possibilities emerges.

One thing is certain: for an architect who uses stone as a building's skin, there is a lifetime of learning and experimentation to be had. A stone structure won't make any of us immortal, but it may be as close as we can come to leaving something of our creativity, individuality, and humanity behind. Perhaps that is the intuitive reason that I find stone the most moving and complex of all the building materials. I have not yet reached the end of my love affair with it, and I don't expect I ever will.

A menagerie of masonry: reclaimed brick mingles among fieldstone, with large, heavy "barn stones" acting as a plinth or water table. The thicker and heavier stones at the base transition gradually upward to smaller stones and bricks.

OPPOSITE: When a sleek or more formal look is desired, coursed limestone makes a wonderful choice. For the home of my friend Richard Tubb, we wanted a simple, modern Palladian villa of antiqued stone in a running-board coursing. FOLLOWING PAGES: Stone offers endless variety in patterns, textures, profiles, and mortar colors. PAGE 118: The change of texture from the chiseled face of the stone risers to the sanded face of the pool coping makes all the difference in the character of this poolside. PAGE 119: All regions have their own indigenous stones. Some are more workable, more shapable, and prettier than others. One of my all-time favorites is limestone from the great state of Texas in warm tones of khaki and cream, as shown on this house we did in San Antonio.

THE LAKE HOUSE

I think it's always important for a house to appear to be indigenous to its context and surroundings, yet also have something unique to say about itself and its inhabitants. It need not shout for attention; it just needs to be confident in its own place, in its own clothes.

I designed this house by the Lake Martin reservoir in Alabama to be similar in spirit to a person you see at a cocktail party and look forward to getting to know. Its exterior feels approachable, solid, and stable, yet a bit different for a lake house. A silver-gray patina warms its cedar shake roof. Its limewashed stone walls unify and simplify the color range.

Adding to the bit of mystery is a walled courtyard (inspired by those I had seen in travels through Central America) with a fourteen-foot gate, perhaps a bit unexpected in this context, a conscious wrinkle in the experience of entry. When the gate is open, the view flows through layer after layer of the interiors—an enfilade being one of my favorite design devices—culminating with the lake in the distance. For inspiration closer to

OPPOSITE: A climbing rose softens the large gated entry from the gravel motor court.
FOLLOWING PAGES: The peninsula-shaped lot allowed for expansive lake views from the swimming pool and screened porch; on the home's westerly side, a bracketed overhang protects against the hot southern sun. PAGE 124: We nestled the entry between the grassed terrace and the porch, with its cypress beams and columns. PAGE 125: The see-through living space offers the visual enticement of the lake.

ABOVE: The walled enclosure of the grass terrace. OPPOSITE: Rooflines of cedar shakes soften the heavy solidity of the stone facade. FOLLOWING PAGES, LEFT: In the entry foyer a simple charcoal stair is veiled with linen panels. FOLLOWING PAGES, RIGHT: Entry-hall greetings: polished stone pavers and smooth plaster walls contrast with the rugged stone exterior.

home, the side-yard houses of Charleston utilize a similar processional device: first a gate, then the porch, then the discovery of the entry. Here, this progression enabled us to create an outdoor space that holds interest without being directly on the lake. Additionally, it gives the house an area that is largely sheltered from the sun, always desirable in the summertime.

Sometimes the architectural languages inside and outside are in lockstep. At other times, a little bit of a surprise in the transition can be really wonderful, especially in more relaxed places like the lake. The exterior here, with its lake-centric texture of cedar and lime-washed stone, transitions to an interior of smooth plaster, more clean and svelte, with sanded beams of white oak bleached a bit to fit into the light color scheme. Like the person from the cocktail party, the house continues to unfold as new discoveries take place and the lake view becomes larger and more detailed. The transparent foyer is petite and unpretentious, wrapped in steel windows, with some of the stone from the exterior to introduce you to the inside. The interior wood is pecky cypress, which has a wonderful, welcoming scent. We used it on the great room's cathedral ceiling and as cabinetry to keep the array of different materials to a minimum.

I envisioned the great room as a space that would, after a passage through many layers, finally make a direct connection to the lake. But we still needed a wonderful lake porch. To join the porch and the great room as one space, a wall of steel windows can fold up and out of the way. (The cathedral ceiling extends out onto the lake porch almost like a barn.) From here, the lake, the dock, and the boat await, just twenty or thirty feet away. If that seems too far to walk, even closer is a pool surrounded by grass, where a cooling dip can be had while staring out at the boats puttering back and forth across the lake.

A soaring great room ceiling meets the screened porch halfway, with tall sections of steel windows that fold away to form one large space for parties.

ABOVE: I love spaces that create an emotion. They can be as simple as a tunnel from a darker space into the light to draw us in, like this Jacobean-style arched opening into the kitchen's brightness. OPPOSITE: In the kitchen, a boldly coffered cypress ceiling introduces an organic element and a strong organizing grid. And besides, a little "bling" never hurt anyone.

Windows are the eyes
to the soul of a house.

Day or night, the windowed walls of the dining room make sure that those
who gather at the table enjoy the lake views and passing boats.

ABOVE: Thinking about boats and nautical things led me to the image of a ship's prow cutting through the water. This idea became a bracketed overhang of carved beams and rafters that helps keep the screened porch shaded from the strong southern sun. OPPOSITE: A steel-framed window wall folds away to the porch, the view, and the large prow.

ROOFLINES

From our powerful, poetic experiences of nature, rocks, and sunlight are born dreams for a shelter of our own, with rooflines sculptured like mountains and smoky stone chimneys like trees. These two inventions together form the home's sheltering crown.

Of all the structural components at our disposal for the creation of houses, roofs are paramount in importance. Their forms attend to our deepest desires for safety and shelter. In the nature of their materials and their sweeping lines are gestures that our eyes follow from the lowest wave to the highest peak. In our roofs lie meaning and mood too.

In striving for design solutions for the roof, it helps to revisit the masters, whether past or present. Lutyens, Voysey, and Bernard Maybeck created swooping, lyrical lines with deceptively simple appearances and surprise dormers and chimneys. In the free-flowing forms and folds of Zaha Hadid and Frank Gehry, there is revelation as roof and wall become one.

OPPOSITE: The three layers of this cedar-shake roof increase in slope as they move toward the sky. Hiding within its folds are clerestory windows that allow diffused light to enter the living spaces from the eaves. FOLLOWING PAGES: Octagonal, hipped, swooped, and shed: this beach house wears multiple hats. The different folds in the roof create interest for the eye, but the overall goal is always to achieve an asymmetrical balance.

The details make all the difference, even and perhaps especially, on something as large and encompassing as a roof. The challenge lies in the editing, for it takes an artist's eye and experience to assemble eaves, rakes, gutters, rafter tails, and cornices thoughtfully into a seamlessly integrated composition. Still, the architect does well to remember that a roof has a big job to do to protect us from rain and sun. I love eaves that are deep and a bit brooding, for they feel inherently guard against whatever may come, be it snow and hail, monsoons and sheets of rain, or the heat of the sun. Dormers always make for wonderful interior spaces as well as punctuations in what can be a run-on sentence of ridgelines. Chimneys rise up above the roof and lay claim to running the place. But the roof, like the mountains, calmly endures, not the least bit intimidated by the occasional peacockish chimney. Thoughtful rooflines, with breaks in slope that flatten as they head down toward the earth, are wonderful, looking rather like a dancer who leaps majestically and lands gracefully at the trajectory's end.

At the micro level are the shingles: cedar shakes and slate as well as tile made from clay or terra-cotta, even copper and zinc. These natural materials bear their character in varied color and texture beautifully. Because of these organic attributes, they fit into the colors of the natural landscape in a wonderful and indigenous way.

What one could say about roofs—the endless design possibilities and great, singular examples—would easily fill a book. The visceral sense I feel about them is this: the roof protects. It gathers in a grand, architectural equivalent of an embrace. The roof, you see, is a giver. We don't replace walls or columns or beams. We replace roofs after they've given us all they had.

Wood-shake roofing and copper details at ridges and dormers on this beach house lead up to a "widows walk," so-called because it was where women supposedly watched for their sea-faring husbands' ships to return home.

143

RIGHT: Wavelike "eyebrow" dormers atop this Shingle-style house in
the Appalachian foothills mimic the mountains in the distance.
FOLLOWING PAGES: So many materials and details are associated with
roofs, and there are endless options for woodwork in
the eaves of sculpted beams, rafter tails, brackets, and corbels.

RIGHT: Adornments of towers and broad-shouldered chimneys emerge from the roof massing of a rambling beach house on the Florida coast. FOLLOWING PAGES: At a fish camp of sorts, a sculpture of rooflines ties together the different buildings in the compound. Low-slung wraparound porches surround the main living areas and protect the living spaces from the harsh sun. The freestanding covered porch is a watcher of sorts that looks out to the dock and lake.

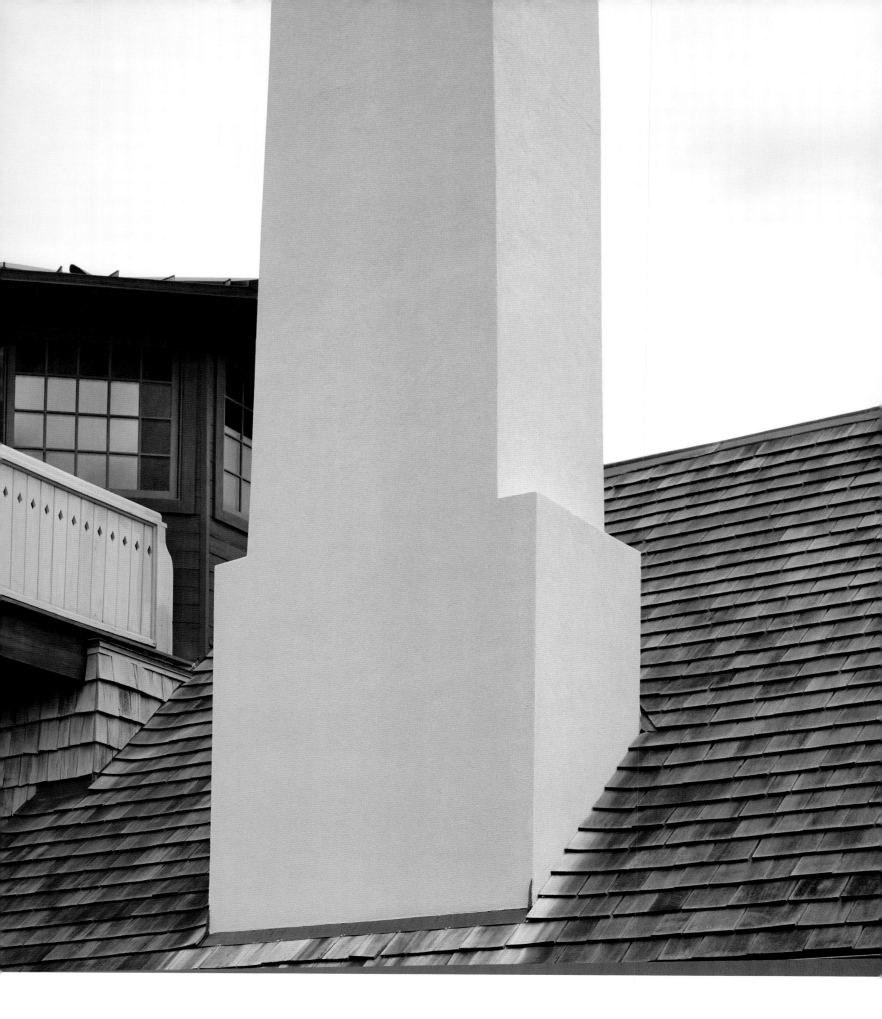

THE CREEK HOUSE

Through our journeys outdoors, we can escape the everyday and find ourselves in the process. Some brave souls among us decide to make that jaunt into nature a more permanent kind of journey. The owners of this home outside Birmingham, Alabama, were of such persuasion. They had purchased a sizable wooded acreage bordering a meandering creek and were excited about living life in a different way.

With thousands of feet to roam in all directions, the decision about where to place the house and the avenue of its approach were infinitely varied. We finally decided to set the house not far from the creek, keeping many of the trees and embellishing the view with an added swath of meadow. The creek's inviting sound and glistening movement were intoxicating. So were its curving undulations, the pools, eddies, and rocky drops that provided inspirational fodder for the design of the house itself. Along the meander's outer edge was a sheer rock face, like a miniature Grand Canyon, carved over the centuries by the water's flow.

In the creek's sinuous mystery, I saw how the house could flow across the site's rolling woodland and meadow. I started to wonder what the water might have to say about the sudden intrusion of something man-made into an environment untouched by man for millennia. In that conceptual transaction, the house began loosely to take shape, its layout an abstraction honoring the creek's natural boundaries and contours. Rather than totally Cartesian or Euclidean in plan, the design evolved to be a bit looser and more organic. The rooms, with their differing functions, evolved into about seven rectangles, arranged to lie rather like the links of a necklace, loosely in the shape of the

OPPOSITE: A river run through it: a minute's walk from the house, a pair of Adirondack chairs create a daily destination by the creek, the landscape feature that gave us cues for the house's overall design. FOLLOWING PAGES: We love using indigenous materials to blend playfully with nature.

Inside the garage's stone tower, a stair climbs to a separate, private guest suite. To the right is a glimpse of a covered pergola, a drive-through that connects to the main house.

creek. The clients loved the feeling of such a layout—a freedom of movement and of the wide-open spaces, echoing a freedom to live differently.

Once the plan was cast, the rest of the house unfolded three-dimensionally as rooflines followed its rhythm. In shape, these upper reaches formed a series of ridges that rose and fell into one another in a natural way. Capping the main roof was a little cupola reminiscent of old barns; the lower ridges spilled out from there.

In terms of style, the architecture used a vernacular that was decidedly informal and in the vein of old farmhouses and barns. (Barns are the warrior-poets of architecture, sturdy and strong, church-like and elegant in their simple efficiency, and confident without being cocky.) The design of this house—only one room deep—allowed for natural light to enter from more than one direction while framing views outward into the landscape in multiple directions.

The entry opens onto the generous heart of the house, a room that combines kitchen and dining beneath softly curving trusses, from which custom steel chandeliers hang on chains. The adjacent spaces offer opportunities for other experiences because we humans are, after all, complex, moody, changeable beings who crave variety. For cozy conversations, we created a small den for two with a low-beamed ceiling and walls entirely of stained wood. A stone fireplace nests in the corner next to a bay of windows looking toward the creek. On the other side of the kitchen, a see-through living room with steel windows on both sides opens up toward the creek vis-à-vis a porch and an elevated lawn and pool—outdoor spaces that serve as connections back to the land. Flanking the ends of the elevated lawn are a pergola for poolside shade and a freestanding screened porch. These outdoor retreats lead gently toward the meadow and woods and, of course, the creek, always on the move, shimmering along the property's edge, its babbling whisper beckoning for a visit.

I worked with Beth McMillan, who was a delight to collaborate with, on the interior design. With this room having such a high ceiling, I felt the fireplace needed to rise as well. We designed the living room as a see-through space using steel windows that allow great views in both directions and sunlight to flow in from sunrise to sunset.

To me, this is a spiritual space. Light flowing sideways beneath a cathedral ceiling of stained-cedar beams makes for a powerful environment, a place consecrated to the simple enjoyment of the natural beauty that surrounds it.

I love interiors that create a sense of fantasy. Of all people, Einstein agrees, saying: "The most beautiful thing we can experience is the mysterious."

A trussed, barnlike space, this kitchen surprises with its steel accents of a large stove hood and a chandelier. And why not? Everyone ends up in the kitchen anyway.

For every yin, there must be a yang. Tucked in under the tall, trussed ceiling is a small, lower ceiling I call the "snug," containing a wood-paneled breakfast nook.

OPPOSITE: The small window reinforces the sense of privacy in a bedroom.
ABOVE: The plastered corner fireplace of the master bedroom.

THE WALL

When I think of the design of house, I think of its fundamental elements. When they are composed in certain thoughtful ways, they create beauty and meaning in our lives. It's impossible to imagine a component of architecture more fundamental than the wall. Of all the tools at design's disposal, few are as useful, more celebrated, and adorned.

The wall supports, and encloses. With a wall, we can create shelter from the outside world. It shields us from physical hazards allowing our minds to escape, to ease us when we come to rest within the safety of the retreats they form.

In its supportive role, the wall is paramount, for as it holds us inside, it also holds the roof over us. As we enjoy the structure of its envelope, we also enjoy openings in its expanse that allow the flow of light and the sun's warming rays within, and that frame our views outward into the world. As we rest in its protection from danger, we also feel the need to pierce the wall to gain entry through a door. So the wall graciously allows us to carve openings into it, offering a welcome as well as a barrier.

With its water wall and masses of stone, this house reflects my friend Dr. Alex Vasquez's native Guatemala. He and I spent a week together there immersed in the culture. The country's historic architecture—its convents and cathedrals, the mixture of stone and brick—provided more than enough fodder for the design, and those memories continue to inspire me to this day.

It is impossible to live well without the security and peace of mind walls give us. But these are all practical considerations. What about beauty and aesthetics? We celebrate our walls as an artist would a canvas. We paint over them using plaster, paneling, wallpaper, fabric, and tile, to name just a few of the hundreds of materials we may use to adorn and accentuate the great definers of our homes.

I consider the design of an interior wall very similar to that of an exterior one. I like to carve into them like sculpture. I love to study each plane alone, as a thing unto itself. In a simple way, a wall has two chief aspects, the solid and the void. On the exterior, I'm interested in playing with the energy and movement that the careful placement of doors and windows can create. The resulting relationships between positive and negative space either please the eye or they don't. When they do, you can turn the drawing of the facade upside down or sideways, and it will still be visually balanced and harmonious. If you have not worked through the relationships properly, though, viewing the composition from any other angle won't make it better. We lavish our attention on interior walls just as intensely, scrutinizing the width of openings, their edges, and their details. We add layers of trim, paneling, cabinets, shelves, art, and drapery. The wall and its proportions, the solid and the void, the material, the detail—all this, to us, makes the wall art, itself.

I'm fascinated by the effect of bringing the exterior walls inside in spots to remind us of what we saw and felt at the outset of the experience of a house. Their continuity provides an echo of those first impressions—their solidity, a sense of safety that helps us rest.

RIGHT: The stone retaining walls of this property create usable and greatly needed outdoor spaces for a site that slopes steeply down to Lake Martin. Horizontal barnwood panels counter the heavy feel of the stone; the verticals of the upper story get much lighter.
FOLLOWING PAGES: Shaping and sculpting curves of limestone or tabby (stucco mixed with crushed shells), arches of stone, and portals of wood—the details and materials we choose for our walls say much about what kind of place we create— beach or city, formal or playful.

Exterior walls are storytellers. Rendered in early-twentieth-century reclaimed Bessemer Grey bricks mixed with antiqued Indiana limestone, the walls of this Cotswolds-style house, inspired in part by the metaphor of an abbey, help create a village of forms that appear to have grown over time. Preserving history, these walls replicate the old brick architecture of the site's previous house.

A QUIET SHELTER

There are houses that are made for ocean or mountain views and those that are for parties and entertaining. Then there are houses that are designed to be a haven, a rest for the body and soul. John Saladino said it well: "A house is much more than mere shelter. It should uplift us emotionally and spiritually." This client, herself so serene, expressed the desire for such a retreat.

Because the client's site in Shoal Creek, Alabama, was wooded, the house by definition was going to be a secret hideaway amid the trees. To become a place of peace and sanctuary, it required an architecture that spoke of safety. For its protective shell, the layout had to feel like a compound yet not appear complicated. The exterior had to have strength and an almost chapel-like quality. It asked for masonry, but I wanted nothing too dark or rugged. Groupings of parapets made of light-toned stucco-coated brick gables provided the shelter, which emerged in the form of a petite chapel house. Sculptural and evocative, the parapets projected up above the roofs to pinnacles topped with limestone. The effect was of walls that had lasted for centuries, like ones I had seen on Irish castles and Egyptian pyramids.

One of the client's few requests was for rooms filled with light. Providing the amount of fenestration necessary to deliver luminosity through the expanses of limestone called for some design trickery, as the glass had to dance with the stone in proper proportion and style. It was also important

Solids and voids play off of one another at the arched entry and chimney
to create a framework for the foyer's clerestory windows.

A chamfered chimney peers over castle-like details, with limestone caps inset from the stucco and copper edges at ridges and gutters.

We used stuccoed masonry to
create a simple texture for the
various shapes of parapets
and plinths. Resolute and solid,
the exterior contrasts with
the more soft, delicate interior.

for the quality of that light to be gentle and come in at different times of the day to create what I hoped would be a peaceful effect.

Feeling assured that the masonry walls would give a sense of security, I set my mind on creating serenity for the interior envelope. I organized the house proper in a linear fashion for livability, with an interior enfilade that flowed simply from room to room. This axial arrangement, rather like the central aisle of a church, was easily understood at a glance and offered ease of movement, both significant spatial factors in creating a sense of calm. It also enabled light to flood in from different angles throughout the day, just as the client wished. From one end of the house to the other, the spaces progressed from most public to most private. A small porch and pool opened to the living room. In the center were the kitchen, keeping room, (meaning a small multipurpose room typically adjacent to the kitchen) and dining nook. Then came the house's most private part, a master wing guarded by two garages and a hidden motor court to enhance the sense of security and seclusion.

The Italians have always said, "If you're tall, you're halfway to beautiful," and it's an idea that also applies to spaces. The long, slender shape of the living room and its high ceiling made for the elegant atmosphere I wanted. But there was still the matter of form and skin to give the light something to attach to. Soothing, organic, contoured shapes came together in a sinuous plaster chimney that became the living room's focal point. Slightly arched and softened openings throughout the house added to the graciousness. To make the interior skin more ethereal, we used a shade of creamy white with a glossy finish that reflected the light with a shimmer.

At the end of the construction, the owner remarked how uncanny this new place was and how perfect it felt for her, and she asked how we had made it so peaceful and serene. I said, "I just tried to make it like you."

The stone exterior gives way to a shimmery plaster interior of creamy tones and simple linen-slipcovered furnishings. I worked on the decor here with Richard Tubb.

OPPOSITE: Layers of light move through the interior enfilade. ABOVE: The petite kitchen has just enough space for entertaining and still feels comfy for two.

Light, bright, and white, this kitchen is probably one of my top three favorites—reminding me that simple is always best.

Nature has been a huge influence on my designs. Its shapes have become the basis for many of the forms in my work.

A chamfered masonry archway frames the view out into the trees while the reflecting pool gurgles its calming song.

WINDOWS

It has been said that the eyes are the windows to the soul. In the design of a home, the windows are the eyes of the house. Like our eyes, the windows reveal an inner truth in the way they transmit a degree of emotional and spiritual transparency. Who, after all, can resist trying to get a glimpse of the world on the other side of the glass as we walk or drive by? Windows tell us much about the character of a place, whether its form is inspired by history or completely modern, whether its persona is more buttoned-up or loose and relaxed, and perhaps a little of what's going on behind the scenes (especially in the evening, when the light inside reveals more).

From the inside, the windows are our eyes into the world. In the hands of a thoughtful designer, they frame a view as if it were a painting. We are always trying to create spaces that have drama and emotion and that leverage the opportunities of their views. For those efforts, windows are indispensable. Often, they are the initial thoughts in a room's design. Frequently, they are one of its most important features.

For me, windows are also about light and its transmission into the interior—and the rendering of form and materials as a result. In two of my favorite places—Antoni Gaudí's Sagrada Família basilica in Barcelona and

A room with a view never hurts the creation of a great experience. For this architect, an occasion to look through a window and see architecture as well as the great outdoors is like looking into a mirror and seeing oneself.

Warren and Wetmore's Grand Central Terminal in New York City—the streaming light makes for a visceral experience because of the inspiring window shapes and their thoughtful placement. Shafts of sunlight flow into the interiors resplendently, angling from on high, with life-enhancing qualities that seem to transform the very volumes created by the walls and ceiling from the everyday into another world altogether.

Architecturally speaking, windows are primary structures in the language of a home. In more expansive rooms, I have come to enjoy using windows in large groups, stacking them on top of one another in rows or with transoms, making entire walls of glass. But in some rooms, one simple window can be just as powerful. Where privacy is needed or wall space is at a premium, a little spot of transparency surrounded by the heft and heaviness of a stone wall has a mighty effect.

Once we get past the "where" part of the window question, I think in terms of details. The size and shape of the panes, smaller (which I mostly prefer) or larger, affect the view of the outdoors. I have long been fascinated by an ancient glassmaking technique, rediscovered by the Gothic artisans, which yields small, circular panes called rondels that are leaded into place. Then there are the shapes and profiles of muntins (the slender divisions between panes). Add into all of this the layering of mullions (the columns between windows). Every one of these components must be thoughtfully considered and detailed in material, color, and shape before the architecture is complete. Of all the things I would say about windows, I will say they are as fundamental to a great house as great food is to living well. Without them, we would not be able to enjoy the powerful views of nature or allow the life-giving force of light to enter our rooms. But perhaps the most important trait of windows is this: they imbue our homes with that most uniquely human characteristic of all—a soul.

OPPOSITE: When windows go from floor to ceiling, sometimes a wall of glass can define a room.
FOLLOWING PAGES: Several of the many ways of making windows in leaded glass.

Windows are as much about what we see outside and the pictures they frame for us as they are about bringing light in. Here, the windows filter a vertical view through trees down to the horizontal lines of a lake.

THE FIRE TOWER

When this client and I first met years ago, there was no project on the horizon, but there was a great reaction. He was fun-loving and intense, with a palpable, infectious passion for life, and he shared my love for design, for how things are made, and for authentic materials. When he called years later about building a house on some property he and his wife had purchased atop a mountain in North Carolina called Laurel Knob, where the views expand for more than fifty miles in multiple directions, I was excited at the prospect of working with him. By then, they had already completed a guesthouse with a wine cellar, a garden, and a chicken coop.

Their children grown and gone, it was just the two of them with their three German shorthaired pointers, surrounded by nature—plenty of deer and a few black bears as well—and quite off the grid. A welcoming committee of barking bird dogs greeted me when I arrived. We walked through the woods to share a picnic lunch at the spot they felt had the best views (they were indeed mind-blowingly good). This part of their property was full of low evergreen trees, laurels, rhododendrons, and wild blackberries.

What resonated most in our conversations was an architectural metaphor (and childhood memories) of fire towers built by the National Park Service in the late 1800s, dotted along the high points of mountain ranges to

I enjoy the breaking apart of a house into smaller pieces that can be enjoyed all by themselves. At the stair tower, stepped windows climb above a menagerie of masonry that fits reclaimed brick and fieldstone on a base of thick barn stones. The stair tower is a good example of making houses with a more approachable scale.

give advance warnings of forest fires. Many of these towers were powerful yet simple structures constructed of stone from foundation to roof, whether to endure forest fires or because the long-gone generation that made them knew no other way to do things than to do them exceedingly well.

Inspired, I flipped over a paper plate from our lunch and started sketching some conceptual drawings. The debate went on regarding where the best view was and which orientation would be optimal for the house. At the end of the afternoon, we had a basic direction. As the design process continued, so did the passion for historical references, particularly for houses from the late 1800s through the 1920s. She, a talented painter and interior designer, had a lot to say about how the interiors should feel. He, the owner of a company purveying antiques and reclaimed materials, employed his talented crew of artisans to craft many of the elements and make much of the furniture.

The limestone and fieldstone of the exterior walls repeated on the hearths and fireplaces, carrying through to the interior the patina of the old materials wrapping the outside of the house. The bluestone pavers on the terraces flowed into the living room and kitchen. The roofline's reclaimed beams and beadboard eaves also echoed within, forming a vaulted ceiling for an upper level focused on the panorama of the Blue Ridge Mountains.

Touches of modern-day design—especially steel windows—added contrast throughout. We used old steel panels from Prague, found by the client, to wrap the elevator shaft in the center of the stairwell in a way that was modern and clean. Gradually, the house drawn on paper plates emerged through the trees to cast its own shadow. Looking back on the journey, it was one big adventure. But we stayed true to our original vision of old fire towers, the shared chemistry of our love of life and design, and the power of transformation that architecture holds.

A bay of steel windows overlooks the entry tower and the welcoming committee of bird dogs waiting at the reclaimed gates.

RIGHT: Steel windows in this bay shape a cozy snug for enjoying the living room and a fireside chat. FOLLOWING PAGES: The crow's nest on the top floor offers panoramic views of the Blue Ridge Mountains. When you have a property—and a space—as special as this, the last thing you want to do is to leave the room. As carefully as possible so as not to encumber the view, we added the comforts of a small kitchen, pizza oven, bar, bath, and fire.

I'm drawn to materials that are honest and make us feel grounded. I love materials rendered in their natural state, displayed in the light.

OPPOSITE: In the kitchen, windows above the sink and a thin steel shelf maintain the visual connection to nature. The polished Carrara marble of the island reflects the wooded surroundings. FOLLOWING PAGES, LEFT: Jeff Sikes, the owner, and his talented artisans carved many of the house's wood pieces on site, including these beams and circle-sawn brackets of heart pine in the upper reaches of its upper floor. It was like instant design gratification. I would sketch some detail with a few dimensions Jeff had requested and send him a picture of it. Many times, he would send me back an image later that same day of the corbel or the newel they had made. FOLLOWING PAGES, RIGHT: Tucked away for loft use, a small bath is handy for guests at parties in the crow's nest.

RIGHT: Half-timbered plaster walls just seemed like the right thing for this mountain home. They're even better adorned with elk antlers collected from the European travels and furnishings and fabrics chosen by owner Maxine Sikes. She has a delightful energy and we had a lot of fun working together. FOLLOWING PAGES, LEFT: Detail of a limewashed corbel, bearing the marks of the tools that shaped it. FOLLOWING PAGES, RIGHT: In the master bedroom, an elliptical steel window surrounded by a padded linen "headboard" filters a little natural light onto the pillows of the master bed. PAGES 216-217: The upper-level porch of the crow's nest enjoys panoramic views of the Blue Ridge Mountains and overlooks a rear terrace, which has radiant heating under the pavers to melt the snow.

DETAILS

When I am thinking about design, my first ideas are of basic shape and form. This is a bird's-eye kind of view. After the dust settles on the site layout, flow of the plan, and the mode and manner of rooflines, another world opens up. It is design at the level and scale of the hand. This is a quieter conversation, experienced face-to-face and close-up. It is thinking at an intimate level and noticed only by the careful observer. The delicate pieces and the details are not for those in a hurry—a casual passerby could easily miss these small yet powerful morsels. There is something magical about seams, about the deep, thoughtful way edges and borders can come together. At this level, design can beckon to the infinite. As Albert Einstein said, "The most beautiful thing we can experience is the mysterious."

In a word, detail is about nuance. It is the finer distinction. It comes from how the smaller parts relate to the larger theme, or how they begin a slightly new language and dialect of their own. I have become captivated by the magical effect when one material comes into contact with another. I am also entranced by the effect of scale, such as when a pattern forms that can only be appreciated up close. For example, I love circles and

No detail of molding, corbel, or handrail can happen without the skilled eye and hands of the artisan. Carpenters shaped this cupola's chamfered rafters and tapered boards by hand, fitting the pieces like a puzzle.

ABOVE LEFT: Sometimes a detail is simply an omission of standard conventions: I love the way the floor meets the wall sans base molding.
ABOVE RIGHT: The rustic joinery of this door made from reclaimed wood fits together raised panels, stiles, and rails. OPPOSITE: A window's grid of panes and muntins creates a play of shadows and light in the stairwell; a stone finial I found at a garden shop tops the newel post.

ovals. I often use them at different scales—as large wall openings or tiny ones, perhaps as the pattern in a vent or in a window—to develop a kind of pattern language specific to the place I am designing.

Detail often has to do with edges, where one thing starts and another ends. I think about the way the window sash comes against the mullion. Both are wood, but one is painted and the other stained. I look for a way of celebrating an opening, with the frame of a limestone surround, then outlining that border with plaster and recessing it slightly behind. This kind of layering, too, relates to shape and form. Picture the shape of a steel window muntin, the chamfered edge of an arched opening, the infinite variations of wood molding "profiles" on a paneled wall. Detail is what happens in an architectural moment, the thoughtful way the transition occurs in the crevice, the curve of an ogee, and so on. As we experience architecture, the surprises that occur along the way are part of the delight and enrichment. The creative options for detail never end, for there is something eternal and infinite held in these edges, ornaments, and facets.

When I was younger, I designed not ignorant of detail but almost intimidated by it. What I learned over time is that to design without it leaves a hole that can't be filled, for we have an innate, incurably human need for depth and delicate layers. So I have soldiered on, grappling with this degree of design at the molecular level. Still, some of my favorite details are the ones where I omit pieces that would normally be present— such as leaving off a base trim at the bottom of a wall where it meets the floor, or creating a reveal there instead—and let the clashing elements show their inherent tensions. These are the little moments where the house winks at you. If you are not paying attention, you could easily miss them.

OPPOSITE: Even structural elements like beams need not be bereft of beautiful bevels and thoughtful design. FOLLOWING PAGES: The opportunities for contemplating design on a smaller scale are endless.

We found this carved limestone quatrefoil from an English country house at a favorite dealer of antiquities and incorporated it into the design.

ABOVE: Cantilevered stairs in a Florida beach house. OPPOSITE: Perforated masonry walls on an outdoor tower in Alys Beach.

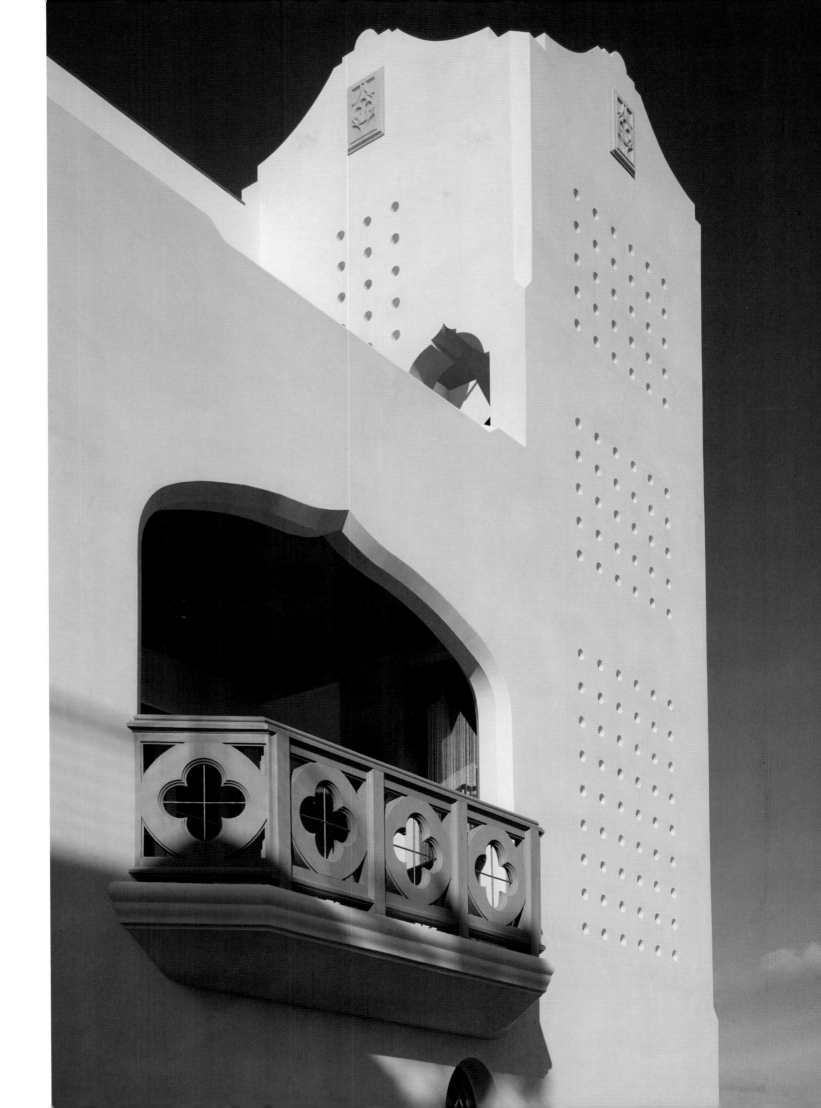

MY HOUSE

After twenty-five years of designing other people's homes, the time came to create one for myself. I wasn't expecting the process to be easy. Ironically, the most basic question—What do I want?—proved the most difficult to answer. The house had to be a simple structure with a petite footprint. I wanted it to be flooded with light. I also craved welcoming, multifunctional living spaces, rooms for my daughters, and a master suite on high. On an emotional and aesthetic level, I wanted a repository for beauty and a retreat.

My steeply sloped micro-lot nestles into a hillside enclave of English-inspired homes on Red Mountain in Birmingham, Alabama, so a vertical structure seemed an elegant solution. Powerful memories of the tree houses of my youth, skyscrapers of Manhattan, and stone towers of Ireland offered an irresistible typology for such a house, a folly of sorts, but one with deep meaning. What ultimately resulted were four neatly stacked stories, easily fifty feet up at the top floor. From such a lofty perch, I could see the curvature of the earth and the city below, and dream.

OPPOSITE: The exterior incorporates some of my favorite materials and my two favorite colors as well. Along the alley, a stone wall encloses a terrace with a small pool, an important design request from my daughters. FOLLOWING PAGES, LEFT: Supporting brackets at the front stoop. FOLLOWING PAGES, RIGHT: A gothic arch frames the front door. I lined my small garden with a low hedge and a row of hornbeams that I plan to pleach together. My mother transferred her love of making outdoor spaces and plants to me.

I sited the house to take advantage of the best views. I turned it at a forty-five-degree angle to true south, which permitted all four sides to capture maximum sunlight from morning to dusk. For the exterior skin, a light, clean, painted masonry, punctuated by cantilevered, charcoal-colored wooden window boxes, felt just right.

Inside, I wanted some moodiness. I imagined a living room that would feel cozy yet bright and simple. Because I wanted a smaller house, I decided to combine kitchen, dining room, office, and living room into one space on the main floor.

The kitchen is the heart of any home, so I started there—and decided to go dark for a change. An antique Chinese chest behind my office desk, gorgeously stained charcoal, inspired the kitchen cabinetry and paneled walls. For balance, flanking the sink with the refrigerator and a tower bar made sense. Along with a lowered ceiling, a wide arch marked the transition between the kitchen and the open, light living/dining room. Folding down the outer edges of the ceiling seemed to wrap the room in a gentle embrace and created a sense of a vault overhead. My dining table-cum-drafting table found a home in a window bay outfitted with a banquette. I carved out a large oval opening directly across the room, exposing the curved stair-rail and allowing in light in midafternoon.

One flight up worked well for two guest bedrooms with a cozy sitting room (in a glassed-in stair-hall landing) for my two younger daughters. With a stretcher table for their homework and white linen at the windows

PREVIOUS PAGES: I worked with designer Betsy Brown on the interior decor. Her quiet, clean style was the perfect companion to my bent toward creating slightly more emotional interior architecture.
OPPOSITE: I love a corner, as opposed to centered, fireplace because it allows the visual connection to the outdoors to be uninterrupted. My leather sling chair is a favorite spot to read and tend the fire.

OPPOSITE: A niche harbors a wooden sculpture from Reunion in Chattanooga, Tennessee. I designed the dining table and worked with the talented Michael Morrow to make it in cerused oak. ABOVE: I use my dining table for drawing more than dining. The comfortable booth seat, sofa, and Christian-Liaigre-chairs were designed by the brilliant Grant Trick.

and covering the opposite wall, this hideaway suited two girls who were becoming young women.

The master suite nests at the top of the house within a space framed by the rooflines and dormers; it is an intimate, lofty retreat that feels like a small chapel in its serenity. A sculptured wall with an oval niche (similar to the one in the living room) provided a backdrop for a custom low-slung bed and headboard upholstered in dark mohair velvet, with side consoles to match. For convenience, I added a small coffee bar at the entry to the dressing hall and bathroom. I used rich, dark materials and finishes in the bath for surprise and contrast, including steel for a vanity and as a frame for the shower and water closet's glass doors and walls. A Gothic vault capped the bath. A privacy screen of rondel glass for the bathroom windows completed the chapel metaphor.

A small plunge pool off the living room, requested by my daughters, increased my options for entertaining and has had a dramatic effect. It also offered other more ethereal benefits: those of sound and reflected light. A little recirculating pipe added movement and music. When the French doors are open, the sound transforms the living room.

My talented friends Betsy Brown, Grant Trick, and Michelle Cone collaborated on the interiors. As with any project, there were things I learned, things I love, and things I would do differently. Those lessons accompany me as I continue my journey.

I had been playing with steel and thought I would experiment with it in my master bath. Since that seemed counterintuitive to conventional thinking in a bathroom, it only made me more interested.

RIGHT: I like kitchens that are clean, unfussy, and full of natural light, not ones filled to the rafters with tchotchkes, nor those that are an ode to cabinetry. A butler's pantry on the far left allows the kitchen to focus on the essential joy of cooking. The windows overlook the garden.

FOLLOWING PAGES, FROM LEFT: Details of the waterfall marble-wrapped island and the softened edges at the archway. Steel framework and fluted glass in the bath. The bath's floor, of character-grade oak. The ceiling arch repeats in the vanity's steel leg. Michelle Cone, who works with me on all of the firm's architectural interiors, designed and built all the steel pieces in the bathroom with her husband, talented metal artist Andy Cone.

PREVIOUS PAGES: I wanted an organic shape to the wall behind the bed, and since it shared space with the stairwell, I designed a large oval opening to allow more light into that space as well as to provide a focal point to the bedroom. RIGHT: The lofty perch of the master bedroom looks out over the city. In my sitting area, Peter Fleming designed the custom consoles, which he calls "Pi" because, like the mysterious mathematical figure, the pattern of door fronts never repeats itself.

ABOVE LEFT: Right by the stairway to the master bedroom, a portiere hides my daughters' television when not in use. ABOVE RIGHT: The bedroom of my two younger daughters, Emma Grace and Tate, offers wonderful views. They share the custom table and poufs. OPPOSITE: My daughters love the light-filled den I created for them at the stair landing to use as a study nook. To maintain peace, each has her own side.

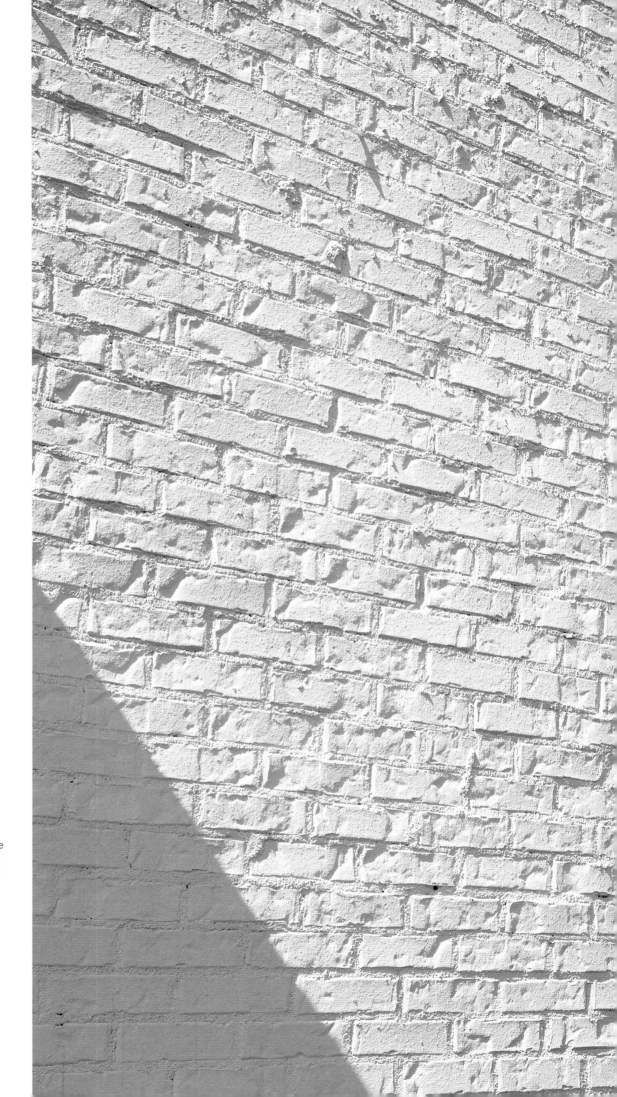

I added a sandy textured mortar wash to the brick so it would blend more into the terrace's rustic gray stone wall that overlooks the trees and the city. I am always attracted to creating things that appear to have a past or a story, that have grown over time or have in some way evolved. The rustic quality of the stone terrace reminds me of old ruins on the moors and fields of Ireland, and the little arched door underneath it seems to me to be something out of a Tolkien novel.

ACKNOWLEDGMENTS

There is a metaphorical yet palpable sense that we can be light to others. In my mind, there's no doubt that I have been blessed by the following rare and luminary people, who have shown me the way along my journey. I have the very good fortune of two wonderful parents, who have bestowed upon me unconditional love and instilled in me a great appreciation and respect for all people. In the end our objects and things will pass, but the relationships we form and nurture will endure. These thoughts I hold close as I thank the many people without whom I would never have been able to complete the works in this book. I would have been a bereft person without the knowledge and wisdom I received from them.

There have been great mentors and teachers along the way whose wisdom has been foundational. As a twenty-year-old at university, my professor Bill Gwin challenged me to think more critically and take things more seriously. I'm indebted to him for, in many ways, teaching me how to think. His wife and fellow professor, Mary Gwin, challenged me to learn how to express myself in words. I fell in love with language and words, which I never would have otherwise. To professor Bobby McAlpine, who inspired me in the quietest ways to think deeper and not settle for the easy (and usually wrong) answers. To my first professional mentor, Alberto Chiesa, who taught me the importance of emotional moments in houses and told me, whenever I was drawing, to "Make it look good, Jeff!" in a heavy Spanish accent that made my given name sound more like *Jayph*. To other professional mentors, Lauren Barrett and Aubrey Garrison, who trusted me despite my youthful naïveté and threw me regularly into the deep end to swim in the practice of architecture and learn. Lastly to my dear friend, and talented architect Louis Nequette, who I had the wonderful experience practicing with for many years and without whom I would not have had the courage to start this journey to begin with—thank you.

I have had consistently wonderful clients on my journey. I have found it absolutely true that without clients who believe in you, it is impossible to do meaningful work. I can never show a great project that did not have an equally great client supporting it. The depth of these relationships dictate the degree to which transparent and honest communication can happen; over time, the level of trust and respect engenders a type of synergy that can do amazing things. My clients have all become teachers and mentors to me, and I hope I have shared with them something meaningful that endures. I have friendships with clients that go back more than twenty years, and for these friendships, and for allowing me the freedom to create probably the largest single investment of their lives, I am immensely thankful.

The work we do is technically arduous and varied across so many skill sets that it is impossible to do alone. Not only this, but it would also be utterly devoid of the joy I experience creating with the talented people I spend most of my daily life with. We laugh and enjoy one another in an atmosphere of respect (and caffeine), using our collective gifts and talents toward common goals: beauty, permanence, and thoughtful delight, to paraphrase Vitruvius. Thanks to my talented team of architects and designers, among them Heath Clement, Michelle Cone, Michael Curtis, Luke Hall, Heather Mims, "Big" Ed Montano, Emily Schmidt, Betsy Shuttleworth, Joel Solomon, Mary Elsa Tomlin, Lindsey Trammell, and Alyssa Webster for the joy on the journey. It would not be half as fun and creatively fulfilling without each of you.

No matter what we design, nothing becomes real without a builder. We are only as good as the builders we work with, who interpret our vision and drawings and samples until sticks and bricks begin to cast a shadow. The magical part is watching the idea transformed from drawings that exist in only two dimensions into a three-dimensional object you can walk up to and even step inside. I have been the benefactor of many great ones, both across this country and abroad. There are too many over the last twenty or more years to thank them all, but a sampling from the preceding pages are Scott Anderson, Scott Barnes, Steve and John Bryant, Don and Mitch Dickinson, Brady Fry, Will Hines, Scott Hughes, Marbury McCullough, Keith Russell, David Sherrod, and Jeff Sikes. You are great builders and men that I admire for your dedicated talent, patience, and vision.

In the world of design, there are many amazing creative people that I have been lucky enough to practice with, including interior designers, landscape architects, lighting designers, and others who have devoted themselves to their particular art forms. I have learned much from them and realize how deeply we need